The Guide
to Being
Bear Aware

Previously published works by SJ Fowler

Poetry Collections :

{Enthusiasm} : Test Centre 2015
The Rottweiler's Guide to the Dog Owner : Eyewear Books 2014
Enemies: the selected collaborations of SJ Fowler : Penned in the Margins 2013
Minimum Security Prison Dentistry : Anything Anymore Anywhere press 2011
Fights : Veer Books 2011
Red Museum : Knives Forks & Spoons Press 2011

Limited edition poetry publications :

Tractography : Pyramid Editions 2016
Whale Hunt : Annexe Press 2014
Vikings : POW 2013
Recipes : Red Ceilings Press 2012
Leaves : VerySmallKitchen 2012
Johnny Tapia : Oystercatcher Press 2011
The Songs of Salvador Sanchez : Red Ceilings Press 2011
Antonio Margarito : Arthur Shilling Press 2010
Klitschko : Zimzalla 2010
Arthur Abraham : Knives Forks & Spoons Press 2010
Poggel Intricate : Writers Forum 2010)

Collaborative publications :

House of Mouse w/ Prudence Chamberlain : Knives Forks & Spoons Press 2016
40 Feet w/ David Berridge : Knives Forks & Spoons Press 2016
1000 Proverbs w/ Tom Jenks : Knives Forks & Spoons Press 2015
Oberwildling w/ Colin Herd : Occasions | Austrian Cultural Forum London 2015
Gilles de Rais w/ David Kelly Mancaux : Like This Press 2013
The Estates of Westeros w/ Ben Morris : Like This Press 2013
Elephanche w/ Marcus Slease : Department Press 2013
Twins w/ Matteo Patocchi : Stuff Press 2013
Primarchs w/ David Kelly Mancaux : Bear Press 2012
Ways of describing cuts w/ Sarah Kelly : Knives Forks & Spoons Press 2012
Art Gallery Bouncer w/ Patrick Coyle : Gauss PDF 2012
Saint Augustine of Hippo w/ David Kelly Mancaux : Kitt Press 2010
Animal Husbandry w/ Sian Williams : Kitt Press 2010

SJ Fowler

The Guide to Being Bear Aware

Shearsman Books

First published in the United Kingdom in 2017 by
Shearsman Books
50 Westons Hill Drive
Emersons Green
Bristol
BS16 7DF

Shearsman Books Ltd Registered Office
30–31 St. James Place, Mangotsfield, Bristol BS16 9JB
(this address not for correspondence)

www.shearsman.com

ISBN 978-1-84861-538-0

Poems in the collection, in one form or another, have appeared in
*Poetry Magazine, Corda, Podium, Poetry Spotlight, Sand, Young British Poets
for Oxfam* anthology (2012) and *Birdbook VI*: an anthology by Sidekick
Books (2016). The poem 'Reluctant Organ Donor' was exhibited at
Jerwood Space, London for the Jerwood Open Forest Exhibition (2016).

Thanks to the editors and curators.
And to Livia and my family, above all else.

Contents

Fear the bear, the bear is real

I know they do not know.
George Seferis

In this universe there are free broken bones
for those who listen to their own songs
without headphones.
It's a better version of speaking
called singing,
which makes the state smooth,
and enters into worlds
of which you bourgeois audiences,
scratching your backs loudly,
remain blissfully unaware.
It's a version of emotions
but only appearing upon the surface,
needing just a glance to be felt.
It's like you pretending you can't be shocked,
just before you are shocked
at the first inexplicable
sound or forced gesture
upon a stage.
Really the state of yourself beyond surprise
is not accessible,
and as a car pours through your living room wall,
so the brickwork falls in,
like a sure sense of justice,
that has just nowhere to go.
It's all a palette after all,
a serious waste of considerable talent,
watching sounds like music
as though they were sights.

Truncatus Tractatus

Everything there is hard on beauty
like a bee draining a flower.
            Sa'id 'Aql

Can someone provide a succinct summary of masterworks?
Your lips give warmth
otherwise denied
but if we get into it, get out.
You block the canal:
for you were born
between the underground
and the ground.
You are pink by volcano half-starts.
To what waters do you take your armour
and your darling?
In what pure spring do you bathe your nose?
You are a cup
full of clear water,
boring.
Rather the high red
with my own breasts like tangerines,
I'll compare myself to taste
and put some real thought into it.
Something stuffed with something dumped.
Flowers and meat,
requiring an expensive engagement ring
makes you an awful person.
This is the lowly tune of a beetle,
no regrets
and I would give life to such a person
if I could make people.

It serves me right to suffer

Duck
she waddles through the dust
in which no fish are smiling
Vasko Popa

From the trouble of the world
comes melting seas
which form land,
from which plants grow
and so I turn
supergrass,
sleeping curled, legs broken, in a cell,
calling for water,
retracting my politics
to eat in various houses
of disaster.
In the hours of troubled memory
before I fall asleep
I remember all those cruel comments online
and the smiling fish
I ate willingly,
descaling their backs
as though I were unwrapping a present.

Bears won't attack me

A friendly history
of vegetarianism,
that which lurks in the shadows.

Livia says bread is in the nose and throat.
Beasts were tame,
when she said that,
tracing back the relationship between food and life,
we see that it stems from a chemical reaction;
sunlight builds up
complex compounds
within plants
which can be used by animals when consumed
and then stored by them;
an energy to grow and breed.

And that's not enough for you;
to see it become a component of fertile soil
the metabolic process by which a living organism
puts off the onset of decay?

Merely assimilating,
from the greek meaning change or exchange,
organisms consume food and exude waste.

Bears attacked me

They're so delicate,
that's why they're those above,
who can't be loved,
asking *why can no one love me?*
Like a blind bear biting my crotch
this evening is a letter of correction.
Sex follows water,
compulsion follows nature
into a magazine.

There have been two marathons to suffer.
One was running
the other a reading.

With two dogs, two female dogs,
I collaborate.
So if we could have quiet debate
for the letter of the sun
that burns permanently
into my brain,
I can say it was a bitch,
surrounded by the suffering
of museums.

Sometimes the story
    like the man who imagines
he is special
 to the prostitute,
        like life,
    goes on and on and on and on so long
you wonder if it's a parody of its own length.

Quietly shown the door

in memory of Tomaž Šalamun

In beauty of awe is the furthest from history
a human can get. But if pressed,
until nobody is coming out from the little cans of the past,
there might be a shift. History is eroded into its friend,
Tomaž, who didn't propel weapons
and wouldn't go to fight.
He kneaded round moulds and inscribed them above the livestock,
like a brand, but not that word, as that word means not what it once did.
He was the one who doesn't pledge the jet (how would he pay for it?).
He bit at the serene health until the great deafness told him
use iodine, dress up, stay put – your double barrel is the clay
and on the hard sand grains grow.
Was he a little torn apart by a length of life?
Of course, lights fuss about everyone,
and each life will have at least one moment of justice between it.
Two dates, that is all it is.
This is him, he went to the store with his wife to buy water all the time.

Grab that nettle

The panther takes its name
from the Greek word for "all" (pan),
because the panther is the friend of all beasts
                    Isidore of Seville

With the world's pounce,
a purple bruise.
Ask those that row
about physical pain?
Ask them, what does it look like?
It has the hooves to help others.
It has the teeth to bite the needy.
It has eyes to see misery.
It has the ears to hear the education
you haven't had.
Meanwhile,
I have had to time to reflect,
don my careful coat,
and claim no eulogy is due for duty.
Draw the dogs who smell the morning air.
Wear black eyes like crowns
in designer skin.
I ask, not for the first time,
make us chase.

It's a legion

You are not the first one – of my women
o, there were many more
but this is the first time, believe me
I've been with such a whore
          Sergei Alexandrovich Esenin

I didn't write the epigraph so don't get angry,
it is not unfortunate that I am associated with lust.
Paramount is shamelessness in the cold,
where it can't and won't happen because it's not allowed.
Get off me too, it's not nice for both of us.
Protrusions become intrusions of course
and then, suddenly, it's a legion,
a friendly party that everyone is telling me they're enjoying
and that I'm spoiling,
by not enjoying.
Then they become forgetful
and in the sack, getting drunk
are like corpses.
As 'friends' speak of 'sleep'
I listen still.

You'll find a bee and sting me with it

I'll book myself a bee-hunting bee
Peter Riley

The length of bodies, stacked end to end,
allows more room
for the numbers to be known by many.
Bodies become rides across the sand.
They get icy.
They become the brick in walls
splitting the lands of a baron,
dividing the museum from the living quarters.
In the court,
there are still those who kneel for mercy.
Still robes becoming entangled in stirrups.
Still people falling from horses.
They land in the mud,
into the ether, namely, that which is not
       and need not be.
That which was once a vision and is now reality.
Knowing that, I tell you,
is a wholly untrustworthy path
for you cannot know what is not.
Our universe with no other purpose
       than its own existence.

Fake black belt in life

and the animals couple frankly
and bees smell of blood, and flies buzz angrily
and cousins play strangely with their girl cousins
Pablo Neruda

Reading reports; that explains it.
Unafraid of death because you haven't thought about it.
Money doesn't control you, you are free from that
like some sort of lion or big cat with wealthy parents.
Accusations of financial impropriety
reflect more succinctly your father's desperation
to talk more and not let your mother rule the house.
I saw all this doing a bad job of your families book-keeping.
Now I live where you visit and in that space I thrive,
treeless, with your sister
where glass lines the floor.
Here I'm having children with myself
and she's watching mate
and there's nothing you can do about it.

Gulo Gulo

We shall kill an animal, but in pity and sorrow
Plutarch

It is an evil chain,
but you're well hungry,
you've been travelling through the body.
Videogames and fried things bar your path.
You furniture a room that's yours.
That's fine, we all need a place to rest.
Misunderstood,
loose in the body,
eastbound in london
but certain in the soul
to build foreign investment.
What is more foreign to a human
than an animal
and its body
becoming fuel for a robot?
On the contrary,
the creature who is bound in its body
but has free organic movements
is tastier,
says the supermarkets.
In the supermarket, I'm free.
The bone of my body is loosened through death,
as vice is through money,
and dietary piety is survival.
Nothing more.

The Tradition

This is how I lost the tournament with my face
Zbigniew Herbert

The trouble with double vision
is that I lose it
right at the moment when it comes in handy.
As though it were friend
whom you remember is dead.
A strange profession, athlete,
where you are more than your work,
and more out of work than in.
Sadness moans
every time a ball is struck
or some other distraction takes place
in physical space.
Not exactly an arrest
but restraining.

All I can say about that

Vapour forth   flamed
shut & digested to mucus
in swan's belly
fish of sky
                    Barry MacSweeney

You're an amazing fish.
You have inseminated the night of my time,
you are the natural enemy of the weasel in my bath.
This is the summation of your sleekness,
a tasty flesh; the opposite of enmity.
You are resurrected good things,
civilisations, bodies unpiled from hot rocks.
It keeps getting better with time.
Our bones together like piano strings that work.
There are deep sea fishes, then there is you.
They love the dark, you are it.
They love you, as I do, a sound out of the depths,
a craked Salome sea monster.

A global ice cream headache

skipping the trouble of learning, abandoning
thought to the wolves,
a nose ring your favourite trinket
        Hans Magnus Enzensberger

In such fair-weather you'll get such friends.
Volume spoiling in the menu.
The clouds gather.
I hate my companions and this destroys morale.
I give up,
I watch for a tall bridge.
The forests I have never seen
are cut down.
Peasant children cannot take revenge
they will birth, when of age, only a kind of conscious bracket,
where they can only be friends with each other
and can only stay where placed.
I am in remembrance,
so please do not sit next to me.
There are other seats,
though I know this is the last thing you wish to hear.
To dislike frailty
and to stuff it down,
deep in the bowels, until it becomes a pack
and uses the body weight of masses to bring us down.

Looper

Why hurry, life, why chivvy on the hour?
You'll soon have time to sew my mouth right up,
stitching with iron threads.
     Olga Sedakova

There are troubles conceiving,
and whether it's exciting anymore,
when it has a purpose
and such fearsome consequence.
Girls in the street look up
and away
even though I'm only looking
because they're dressed as mummies.
Or maybe I look disgusting,
feeding myself apricots
like a pharaoh.
But they were grown from wings
and soon rot on the feather
if you don't eat them in bloom.
Maybe they look away
because I'm ugly,
like a lizard.
Or because I live in my underwear.
Or because of my fertility.
Or because I can regenerate limbs
Or because I insist on tickling everyone.
I'm a good lover though,
I get really nervous.

Aren't you the lucky one?

Culture is elitist by definition
Joseph Brodsky

The difficulty is the loss of memory,
but thumbs are good for keeping records,
compressing buttons.
I am clearly a room,
one of four faces
admitting
I'm a human face now defaced.
A pigboy
with fierce form at the back.
Which do I put forth?
The knuckles
through nettles.
As an animal past it.
having fulfilled lives.
That's why we replace me,
as I would die of old age
otherwise.
I'm sorry your life has been so rough
being surprised
by harm.

Mother's (a baby deer) funeral

And shall we have to deny you then,
God of the tumours, God of the living
Salvatore Quasimodo

I demand help.

It was coming
tranquil threat
jeering because I'm crying.

A few
words
her
Sensible
moon heart
goes gladly
after cancer
crab,
clips a time
of toughness
and constancy.

I read seneca
for my sisters and brother.

I'll not be an animal
they get no ceremony
for their ruins.

Bye bye.

French Exit

alone with the alone
                Plotinus

Hunger is the best cook,
its short range
roving
taste
pleases the softest palette.
That is the lowest common denominator.
The retinue
of folding chairs
who'll follow you,
if you let them,
giving news
of how right you are,
of how they were the ones wrong.
Promises like leather gloves,
embarrassing,
like sunglasses indoors.
A ships sails in,
with a tricolour flag.
A wolf falls into its pit.
Through sheer graft
a person forges
happiness like a dry dock
without time
for spying on their love.

Pap

Love comes but once, can't stay – and when youth flies,
she flies with it – she flies to someone young
Nahum Babad

You lift your dress into a bed where no one has called for years.
My warning is an Instagram video of a child and an owl,
and yet you lie down, say *I'll look at it tomorrow.*
Fuck that, look at it now.
Food waste feels good
you say, struggling
with a mousetrap.
My neck can lap youth I reckon, let's test that out.
When you're sleeping I think
younger people are in flight
from our useful data.
Allow them to lodge in your bed,
at least they won't be used to you,
and having nothing to compare it against,
will not think its deviant or outlandish.

Hive mind

The poetry of the earth is never dead
John Keats

Until you kill it.
The offer of a human massage is not without a price,
hard to find an affordable touch in London.
Tires do nothing to halt now,
like a peace treaty not worth the paper legs that carry it home.
Kindnesses at the races,
people new to betting are given tips.
The locals are welcoming but do expect you stay.
It's a waste of time otherwise.
For they walk the last yard
on the last day of the summer holidays.
You are just a visitor
in the most charming of places.
They have a right to be suspicious.
Your problem is a lack of imagination,
you cannot imagine yourself hungry
or being beaten, savagely.
You cannot imagine how easily
your siege might fail.
They have food enough inside for years.

The Robin Hood Estate

12 foxes thumping; rechristened people.
The Elizabethan Underworld as a precursor to the furnished.
In the year of the calm fox, girls.
The heavyweight watch just to see the mechanics
of victory, that is, as above, a precursor to a tradition, changed into
      a cartoon.
The furry, soon to be protected from insults, or humour at their
      expense, in law.
The drawn fox, the heavy hippo.
Ambush, false witness, poor translation.
In the pressure going down, blood, bicep cuff.
Correction, the neighbour is ill, a shame about the lion
but there remain frequent accounts of premature burials
and lack of perspective so unforgivable
to transform.

Reluctant organ donor

The forest is such an aggressive environment
David Rickard

Striking against the wall,
every inch a row
of quarter bones
quieter than wood.

Interned order of memory,
a place of rest.
Pure construction
repeatedly measured.
Supple like those departed anatomical apes
who linger at right angles,
whose dissection is woe's reward.
Take a seat

Lemon Party

The furious animal swallows its own halo.
Horacio Costa

Firstly
a great length
of trade.
Shake off that cancer,
will the tumour
into a hard blue rock.
Like fame.
Which grants the possessor the power
to defeat disease
as though it were a competition,
and not a flood.
Can we wander about museums without a guide?
What is the German word for that?
What various artefacts add to our regret?
Taking in the immense grandeur of reconstructed skeletons,
bemoaning the massive destruction
visited upon populations over the past century
while threatening species
with smell
and muscle.
We're alike you and I,
you're hungry, scrawny, rude
but we both take the reigns.

Doing coke on the treadmill

A historian is a prophet in reverse
F.E.D. Schleiermacher

Nothing particular or significant
behind the eyes,
rather that which meets the optic
in the world
finishes off the
experience
to make it something conscious.
Or an ocean,
if your poetic imagery
is a wish for love?
Track through
the swamp of recent rooms,
where poets were the same
as you.
Has that conscious experience changed?
Two people
in two days
have used the phrase spirit of the stairs.
And people say the world is getting worse?
Our period is a tidy lagoon,
a tower that will prick the sky,
first building on the foundation of mud
hardened by the united
arab emirates.
For he that is jealous
          is not in love with mud.

Ye Ye

There is no spectacle more agreeable than
watching an old friend fall from a roof
Confucius

Take note of priests in a playground
and other statistical dangers.
A disposition to truth while growing awareness
like a tumour, that sometimes truth spoken
creates lies around the eyes.
Can you envision me in a collar?
Of course you can, you're reading a 'collection'.
Remember I was a pet of girls,
and never fought when taken.
My head drew a draught of Jesus
and my heart lay with his leviathan,
thinking the whole time about
how untrue a thing can be.
There is air enough in water
that you'd think, on paper,
that it could be breathed.
Then you jump in whispering.
His sawdust guts are holy.

This bear is made of felt, stroke it

He even went to sleep without unmaking the bed.
Ana Rosetti

The wall found herself
as a monument to me.
She agreed to it.
Yellowness,
for I may appear
but I am in fact
born unto the wrong body.
Bound
and land where softness is deep
and mind your amusement
for it might offend
those who will eat bone
if only they could get through skin.

Pact

—O Yahweh!
their killer dogs looked us over with curiosity
—O levi baaram batzi Tzion
in a strange land!
                    Genrikh Sapgir

Each muscular dream
of each muscular
body
increases the fear
and shortens the lead
on the lease of life.
Camp blueprints
show seventeen huts
built on the downward southern slope
of the rubbish tip near Clichy-sur-Seine.
Their children are so beautiful,
is it wrong to dream of them
before they're cleared?
There's dogs to rely on,
songs to smother.
Let's be having you.

The best years of your life

be sweet smelling if you love me,
be foul smelling if you forget me
Juan José Romero Cortés

Your intelligence is the reason you're confused,
for if I am abused fingers, as you say,
why are my hand prints so perfect?
I make buildings spin,
houses slide into mud,
river raging, but I hear you can speak to fish?
Melancholy paced
and towards it,
people stood.
It can penetrate baby beakers,
making growing teeth
hurt in their gums.
To grind them down like living,
to make stubs of fangs,
to bite tongues in sexual frustration,
the years of possibility are dying
and longing grows and comes to ask
why am I immortalised?
Dumb to death, it grows
and while we want the ebb of dumb death,
deeply dumb death descends instead.

Pantera

so as I said I am not a cat I
am a red and a green this time
to stay the year...
         Jeff Hilson

Five minutes alone and some think it easy to tell right from left
but when you're obsessed with the five senses,
at the detriment of the seventeen others,
like balance,
one tooth may appear heavier than the other.
I'm quicker to the tree
than you are reaching for your rifle,
so discombobulating is forest navigation
like the risk of being disembowelled
from a distance
by an unkind word. Or is that not true?
It may appear I have withdrawn
into the tit of my mate.
A belly taste in the kitchen,
a tongue thick
with fur.
I would rather be hairless in a foreign place
than leave your side again.

Husky bear

I love you for all the women I do not love
Paul Eluard

Sad enough to tear the battles
that have yet to happen, or have been forgotten?
I've two days in Russia, what is must-see?
That music's broken here,
and two weeks later the pain will still be sharp
You will learn to resent what you cannot learn to live without.

Alyosha, my guide, didn't even say shut up
as I kept talking and talking because I was panicking
because I hadn't slept in days and they tried to take my passport.
Yet out we went, went I, to see her, trying not to complain,
for this is Russia.

I enjoyed it so much, I said *I'll come out to see you again.*
Let us go, she replied, *to bed. I want to dig.*
I am a boar, I said, *I don't drink perfume*
I want to save the earth from the ocean, she replied,
though it is all shit, not afraid or grateful.

We both know you're interested

in which pushing aside the finest grass of the fog
you stroll quite clear
joining hands
          Aimé Césaire

Every time we visit a little village
a brown energy,
it has to be said
let's move here.
Testicles ache in country
like an elephant graveyard.
A freedom
which makes one unhappy,
to speculate.
Working into a frenzy
in the forgotten pubs of a city
that's new to those who have recently arrived.
But having lived here, in the city,
I can tell you no one really lives in the village
and speaking of the old days
the village was immediately underground.
Its where the peasant revolt started after all.
What do you know of that? Memory like a river.
A voice echoing from History, its Arthur Bryant
favourite historian of the prime ministers.
The hog, his dog, old and feeble
is like a famine among young people.
I've decided I'm in between you, breaking
up the fight.
To watch on
as others consent
to their opinions
with the dignity
so unnatural to the opinionated.

You're basic larva

(Spare us from loveliness!)
H.D.

The standard
of understanding
matters
is knowing
all that is
will be
not.
I am no longer able to share fraternity with nature.
Easy on my plate,
easy on the train, easy to bed,
easy to sleep, easy to think.
Easy on the eye.
Rock bottom.
A lamb of nod.
A gum chest,
sick of distrust
I am
nothing
that lies as easy
as others
speech.

Go on then

The gods breathe
Hermarchus

The fat squirrel is a cartoon
on the bookcase of ornaments.
I don't respect the princess of Brompton cemetery
fitting the coil to skull;
the cherry deposits fundraisers,
rolling behind the bookcase.
The Mann family help to search to no avail,
as they're the past.
We're too large to search ourselves,
too heavy to hook,
we've done too well, ruined success.
One piece of advice?
Collects the spores and pillows from hotels,
you never known when you need them.
Also tuck in the shower curtain of your boyfriend's melting fur
and fashion an enormous spoon
that you'll display proudly,
and call your 'éyebrow'
to scoop up the cherry deposit mentioned earlier.
It'll be done.
I'll owe you one.

The Cat-lover's disco

> *gotta lovely pussy cat*
> *& gonna*
> *& gonna*
> *feed him his whiskers*
> Sean Bonney

You're sad and you know you are.
Women who don't like working with women
       admit to me they don't like women.
This is uncomfortable.
It's not my fault the girl is not a standard
but a night time bus driver endlessly lapping suburbs.
Just like me.
One can travel the world
yet to see those beaches again,
its like one has never left the shore.
A bear in Canada tongue licks for blood,
like skin off with sweat imprints that hang in puddles
on the backs of its food.
Or, if you like, victims.
Bend does a pussy leg when landing from on high.
Angels piss in the mouth of the sensitive,
purring and falling.
I'm sorry about that,
wishing it wasn't so acidic like vinegar, the only thing
that'll clean up that rash that's spreading
from your belly button
to your knees.
You'll have to give the cat back,
you're allergic.

Ghosts in the basement

Renovations at the local morgue,
uncover a tourist map
that leads directly to your house.
They take the group down your stairs
and ethereal hands gently press through the wallpaper.
Plaster flakes.
You see reflections of previous residents in the eyes of the visitors.
You find them dropping like flies onto a floor.
Turns out the basement was a room of learning, a surgical theatre.
In the middle was a table of experiments.
Until I found this out
I thought I had commissioned the basement through builders.
Turns out the ghosts got them.
Afflicted friends went slow,
and it was awful,
wishing they had never been born.
The cold air in their lungs
and the locked gate in their hands,
that which one day will greet us all.
I can imagine them down there,
nearly slipping,
trying to find their way around the dark,
doomed, scrambling to the last,
to find a padlock.
And some say, on getting out,
I knew we would never get out alive
and see the day once again.
I don't know about that.
For here we are, outside
lucky to be alive.
But people always find a way to ruin it,
getting used to whatever they've got within minutes of having it.

Nature fascism

there stood the Irish Elk,
a ponderous machinery of pain,
a purposeless castle of gristle
        Ted Hughes

A hammer made of melanoma.
Features on the word landscape aged
by alcohol, for which you are responsible.
Anew gated, and foul.
Your daughter will be my nail.
An electronic voice repeats instructions
six or seven times, you are unworthy,
but its just a fartlek test in the Brittas empire.
Some smile, some drip, some write
of the things they've seen in nature
that were slow enough
to let themselves be seen.
The elk? Just a foreign, massive drunken deer.
The landscape capture on a phone camera
and altered with a paint filter
makes nature beautiful again
The animals appear like suggestions.

Landowner

> *The child thinks the zebra is an animal*
> *The zebra is a vegetable soap*
> Carlos Oquendo de Amat

My moods aren't seasonal,
I keep horses
and they're affected by emotions.
At times they are left to tend
to their own stabling,
as I'm imprisoned for a stabbing.
This is because I've chosen to fight.
Whether to impress a mate,
or define my property.
There are boundaries,
lines in the field
that may not be crossed.
My insignia is a winged horse
starting on a unicorn.
My house is a source of wealth,
the bricks are possessed.

Razorbill

A mason times his mallet
to a lark's twitter
          Basil Bunting, *Briggflatts*

Birds, in their war on woman and man, have failed.
What is left to them is the abject criticism of bread
and the sinking feeling that what is below the water
is as timid as what is above.
Climbing down the cliffs, the bird leaves an envelope.
The letter proves to contain only the statement
"If I can revisit any earthly scene, I should choose the Valley
in which rests the pond and trees." The Razorbill reads this,
hates the cliffs and tries to jump from them.
Out by shot, another specialist gone. A colonial seabird,
monogamous, primarily black with a topically white underside,
a spokesperson for protection – the rarest suks,
watching an Australian film about a killer pig
because their names are similar.

Foo Foo

and I even bite the fruit of your two nubile breasts
to find, in their swelling nipples, god
marvellously transformed into clear honey
Gonzalo Escudero

A winged dolphin
playing a violin with its face.
Its watery mouth is full of bow.
I hope one day
this maddening flesh will be respected,
be airlifted too,
like a climber in the winter
who has doubts.
I lift fish from between my teeth
for too long have I heard
the skull swim.

Thick as a brick

Chokes in the jungle of my arm
DJ Enright

The oration of sand is unending.
Let's all be glad we don't live in the desert,
repeating stored water from the first spillage
where no spear can pierce
slack amniosis
and forced from the first finger thirst
that will dry times like a past punishment.
This is the worst weather
I have ever witnessed
and it's unusually inconvenient,
said sat in the window
of the holiday inn,
eating your favourite,
sorbet
with weeped cream.

A spoken word rhyming cameron with hammerin

and I imagined little details
sheepswool caught in the thorns
red berries
and a prophet's dead face on the pillow
Herbert Read

I see a roundhead that looks like a donkey, and it's talking.
It's enough to imagine a better place to be,
a better way to say maybe it's too bright.
You can hear crying when it stops.
There's O'Keeffe as a heroine disdaining political art,
which she finds illustrative and lowbrow,
not interesting or different from the room itself.
Fill my mouth, I say, should you find me complaining
of gentrification while moving, years from being shrewd.
And that's me. An I. Who listens neither too keen or remote,
as is required for my job as an arts programmer.
And in a certain, recognisable rhythm, to a swaying crowd that claps,
it is though we're dead already.
As though people are already dying,
as though graveyards were full of people who were once alive.
Fate inhales this departure, the politics of speaking words, obsessed.
How fortunate we are to have had your news.
It was as though I hadn't known what you had said before you said it.
As though the kids were never born, the notebooks burned,
with nothing left but ribbons and a scorched silhouette of a powerful
        thing,
laughing at us.
Pay this shadow no mind, you say, it'll rain soon.
Any day now. Any moment.

You need to get that checked out

From childhood I have always loved the mole
because he wears a coat of velvet fur
　　　Constantine Dmitrievich Bal'mont

Hairless dog accompanying the souls of the dead on their journey
underground,
where unlike
the dead
they fossilise
 without air.
To hang from tits
　　　like a velvet
　　　　　blindness
is the dream
of all teenage men,
and though hanging blind,
　　　with neither cane
　　　nor middle-class canine,
can seem dark to the young,
there is sight enough
　　　　to see all is dim.

Stay out of this Max

I don't want to know about myself.
Clemens Schittko

I like, like turtles, to encroach slowly. I'm like a metal chip.
A text which resembles a translation of what happened in that room.
We piled into bomb shelters.
When inside, we maintained focused interiority about time.
It was easier to take criticism from the tribe in good humour, in the dark.
Don't drink poison, don't worry about the monastery, you said.
Its play ball, or don't play.
I say *you can say what you want* in the subtext, but not the text.
This leads to an awkward moment
with a minor bad person shouting at what they deem a major bad person
which makes them appear as that which they're shouting at.
This all seems true and we've met about that and that's resolved then.
The main issue after all is not telling other people how to think.
And you cannot tell how they take what you say anyway, I say. You agree.
In this place *provocative* is a misused word for intensity
by those who are scared of being hurt and so hurt others.
It's as if *intensity* is directed at an internal soft civil war
                              everyone pretends not to notice.

Kangaroo pouch

And then my tragedy seemed greater than the woman's, and I forgot her.
Jon Fante

Argentina, where they pioneered shock
is actually really nice.
Of course they are exceptions.
Does a mountain allow a killer to sunbathe upon its peak?
Yes, it always does,
its a mountain,
cold and permanent
and doesn't care if you've killed someone.
Only you care about that,
and the justice system
and the court of public opinion.
But all that is relative to the society
that houses these mere ideas,
and all that within history,
and history is a recent and also relative
concept.
So were you to kill someone
and be able to be fine about that
unpicking the jesus threads from your wrists
well a mountain would offer you
the same ledge as I,
who has killed no one.
I have hurt a few people though,
but that's not worth feeling bad about,
they deserved it,
and would've done the same to me.
We all need time to repair our cactus
while lesser birds fall, surrendering
in boots outside.
After all, like you, they cannot hope to hear
the street
unless their ears are ringing.

Will you do me a kindness?

the pog
qarks
        Ernst Jandl

Crippling worry and social anxiety,
but still eager
to actively shake the fence.
I'm with your parents, you're important.
It is that we lack secrets within our self-hated
because getting it out automatically makes it better?
We know this from the present.
A character chronicle poorly spelled out
growing from ivory tusks,
like a stripe.
To a beam
balancing
frog person
awaiting poison flames.
You are one of the few gelatine survivors
with toxic glands
who swells with vanity.
To douse you in an accelerant
and walk off
is not possible.

It's only fair

And the crow shouted back: "Crow yourself!"
Daniil Kharms

I maintain imbalances
though I may return balance to imbalance.
I replaced bad for worse in an androcracy.
I introduced subincision
in which the passage is cut
so that the organ can be opened up longways
and pressed against the belly.
I am adopted freely so we might arrogate ourselves
wisdom of our own free will.
A gylanic secret society is formed
which has no leader.
Or so a leaflet says.

I'll take what's going

nevertheless it can hardly be said with certainty
that god prefers a single man in all respects
to the whole of lion-kind
           G.W. Leibniz

A map to very little.
We are a property plan
with illustrations of two dead towns
people have left
for good
to spit spit into mouths of the city.
They now speak a language adapted from
conquest by arguing
it is their duty to convert.
I fought with the Spanish
against the natives
and took part in whatnot.
But that is not contemporary
and other things are.
I say to them,
what memories you have.

No disrespect but

the cow is her bereavement
ranging over the green meadows
knowing the print of cloven hoofmarks in the earth
Lucretius

Tea's good for health like chilli
but you don't see me sticking it
to each of my teeth like a natural whitening agent.
There's layers to this,
the things you're saying are being noticed,
even recorded. I've lost someone.
But I hate that phrase because they're not lost.
I know exactly where they are.
Hong Kong misses me.
I've annexed the cow of China to milk.
I'll be able to shower in liquid.
They'll still be in the same place.
A battle is won, things have changed since they've gone,
bullets sold as souvenirs,
fillings for my teeth covered in chilli.
Besieged for nearly a year with headaches,
I learn to let go.
Collery wins all the prizes
no friend of daylight, no silver mount,
my dvd is no longer available to buy online.
The lost one maintained my PayPal.
They're gone and I must resurrect style,
myself as a Lord of Europe taking money from the queen,
measuring rats in the air with my fingers,
walking nearly 20 miles in a day,
mumbling about Blenheim,
playing a gaggle of ugly fucking instruments,
protecting my rear,
swatting flies.
They're not lost, they're gone.

Thank you crocodile

A young man
with a shaved head
shouting into a mic,
that's what people
think Serbia is like.
Instead of a
blue river festival,
saint sava,
free pancakes,
indigenous abandoned squat fires,
a red harbour
and no chairs
over dirty laundry.
Not in charge
when they ask me on stage if I'm glad
great britain has left its continent.
The velvet centre of censorship
is solidarity.
I'm sick I say
to murmurs from the crowd
that are partially pro putin.
I'm not going to sleep
again.
It's too hot here,
time startled
making the floor cry.
Thanks crocodile
see you next time.

Don't explain the jump

The knowledges and unknown skills of other people
never to be taken for granted
       (in memory of)   Lee Harwood

A wonder
some know how little some know
of the damage
I cause.
I am one of the few knowing only one road
to where the real action is.
Not in nature
but in wires.
The nervous system of human communication.

A stroll through history

To be silent in seven languages
Max Schneckenburger

I wouldn't presume to notate the minutes
for those who can't be with us.
What a meeting.
This evening I am sure our assembly will interest them greatly,
Perhaps I am being pessimistic?
On my way here,
walking through Queens wood
I came across two dead bodies,
which by itself
would be unremarkable,
but the other,
just five feet away from the first,
was an owl.
Still like a cylindrical tonton coffin
who had to flee from Papa Doc Chevalier.

Animal protein

When you have finished your job
then you sweep the floor
don't sweep up children
don't kick the piglets!
          Larin Paraske

A bandage made of sores.
Sweeping through hands to toil and turn to where the eels boil.
Is there nothing that will finish my food?
To its death goes every creature,
in its own sack,
its mother off to town in a nice wooden box.
To the neighbour with the refrigerator,
I will to store 100 frozen pangolins.
Men in china need their scales to recover prowess.
Is it a wonder that we must hack and cough through skin
          as though we were hatchets all dusty and salty?
You must and I can twist mushrooms into meat,
turn kisses into disease,
turn the bolt into brain.
The medicinal snack into your favourite aunt.
I fear with a lack of vitamin B12
it's needed to keep my face fat with worms.

Formaldehyde

*It is autumn. Swans devour the bread of their masters held
together by tears*
                Kurt Schwitters

This camera is great.
I assume I power it with my faith, or is it a robot?
The magnifying glass is meant for looking
like eyes.
You would not burn an ant
with those.
A rock.
A cup of water
All these are fingers and hands
built to discover cracks
and they are all I need
to clear a path
of dirty bathwater
and swim
sunburnt
to the latrine
that has no roof.
For example, I think you're ungrateful
because of how much others suffer
without complaint.
This house in the countryside is great though.
Did you make it all yourself?

The piazza and the flaming orange trees

In the public forests of a single hemisphere the cry of the cock
also known as the nightmare of lions is the place of words
Gerard Mace

Lions sit at the door of their hut staring,
says Tom.
I don't think so,
I don't think they own the hut, I reply.
After that there's improved accusations that I'm macho.
Really, still? After all that pink,
doing penance with fruits and veg
and people I fall over in the street
whom I'm trying to help?
It's still macho to be enthusiastic
and really scared of physical confrontations
for different reasons.
But it's all years ago,
like being chained to a radiator,
it's not real until you start talking about it.
I suppose also its all relative,
      what you think is masculine,
      and what you think is confusing
     or grim.

The Marianne North Gallery at Kew

who was it saying—I remember now—
that there was no forest, probably no jays
(or was it woodpeckers?)
　　　　Alain Robbe-Grillet

Right you are.
There's travels and there's doubt.
She resided in clearing the world that's growing out of the earth
and if a woman like her cannot see the pulp of being
how may I, a trumpet, be of the world of beings?
Giant sloths, apples, Karl Jaspers himself,
all willingly surrender blood for the needy,
thin and albumened, to quench the thirst
of the damaged,
our eyes a Blutkitt animate,
surrounded by pretty plants
feeling overwhelmingly guilty.
We've had some days together.
It was servants that gutted us,
unable to break off individual incidents of the past
from their general corpus.
A dermis lined with lye,
a cored skeleton of steel wire.
An independent wealth who packs depressions with powder.
It becomes paint as it touches water.

I called Ciara Allen's Swamp Monkey for years

Tolerance cannot seduce the young.
    EM Cioran

When I was wetting my bed I was trying typography
and pinning things into the corner of my room,
happy to see them pinned.
I made you not proud.
You would wince when I tried to swing.
I regret certain aspects of my behaviour.
I wasn't nice, but then I haven't only known alone
and now is no different.
That is why.
As I did then, I'd drink your blood again,
because all that has changed is the circumference
and not the centre. It is too late for that.
I don't drink wine, I'm a policeman.
I am an uncle.
I like to dance
around the bones
that protrude from graves.

Tuxedo Surprise

I often regret having come into this petty world.
Erik Satie

Life was brief, gumtree held my attention
and as the whirlpools sided
I saw the talent.
Waiting like fish, waters calm,
I tried to return from whence I came, but that passage blocked.
I wasn't able to join the 'special group' school had earmarked for
      Oxbridge.

It's night, toward the exit,
like the poetry that no one reads, even other poets.
But aside from poets, the bears were on their way to everything at once,
their faces expressionless,
against time running one way, against elite education,
to blame my working class parents for not knowing how that all worked.
The circle keeping shape.

The adults provided me with an insight into the future.
Tormenting for fun and money by singular virtue of possessions.
It does seem better to have a reason.
This is my future.
Peeling uhu from my penis, to feed.
Setting fire to wicker desks
being fired up like glue in the sun,
serum to the pure whack a moles that invade the garden.

Complaining to the cold lamb before its slaughter
is a pretty severe welcome
for those who share its knowledge of life.
This is a limited analysis,
an anxious wringing of sweating fingers,
for in the summer, we all wish to be shorn
and travel unknowing to the coming block.

If you only knew the complications
of living in a stately home, you'd stay indoors.

The Great Bear

Peace be with you, said the blood to the fat flies.
    Jerzy Afanasjew

The bear has a stump as a tail.
The bear as a constellation that looks down.
The bear quadrupedal, the earth's best mammalian killing machine.
The bear skim reading the guide to life in six languages.
The bear is my middle name.
The bear descended from a common ancestor.
The bear as dawn, 20 million years ago, the size of a terrier,
The bear as the language that leads the living forest of the north.
The bear murmuring all grass is flesh.
The bear as some words I won't dare call a poem.
The bear blonde, populous, happy to see you worry you're food.
The bear has paws with which you might measure, in awful size, a
        human scream.
The bear to see fat white blubber exposed.
The bear seeking seals, for it to flail and tear to pieces.
The bear as paper, beyond fearsome to awesome, a good friend.
The bear with a patchy sun belly, rubbed with sand.
The bear is a white sickle moon.
The bear as a burning hammer, stomping but completely thoughtless.
The bear a fur bag in need of claws.
The bear with a specially shaped mouths for insects.
The bear mistaken for a giant sloth but moving too often.
The bear is the animal embodying fear of an eclipse.
The bear is a whole country of people running.
The bear is our son the sun bear that kills more than most
The bear growling to make it worse.
The bear like a group of people talking so that you can't hear them.
The bear comes through tent like a cake through a lobster.
The bear sees crows lift their wings to give the signal.
The bear who wants to be tickled.
The bear who growls *you should have left when I arrived.*
The bear on a bike is as far as the human imagination can stretch.

Vlieland

Peeping out at me from the seaweed was the face of
something rather like a mouse
Inagaki Taruho

To deny the effects of caffeine one must curtsey before reality.
One must holiday at camps, on islands,
that are only above water because of an engineering
no child can really appreciate.

Children, they are everywhere you go,
and might be likened to how it was with fish,
on land,
before overfishing.

It rains here too, and there are other problems,
bringing sand from the beach into your tent, for example.
Never really being clean like you are at home.
But making new friends.

But I am home, and I read children have jumped the water
and swapped with fish.
So the land is nowknown for its deadly enmity,
and attacks without fear of reprisal.

Beast

A halal axe falls on anaemic chickens
Robert Sheppard

In addition to highlighting a desire to charm,
seeing and saying, you aren't being harmed,
no matter how much you repeat you are.
This happens to be the title of a diary,
I am being oppressed.
This is the latest title of *Beau voir* itself,
which of course, contains eight letters.
This is no inadvertent or contingent detail with the reading
experience
figured like a day spent wandering around a somewhat unusual
zoo.
The animals here are hardly in captivity, they are an art gallery.
Few zoos feature glowworms or, for that matter, cats,
and the dodo, of course, is extinct.
One dodo, the foreign visitor,
the ticketless wonder, is ready to scuffle
with lonesome animals in the bucket of sand,
suspicious of prolific poets
because they've not heard of film
or hard work
and think everyone thinks themselves literally a priest,
apart from them,
because it's never their fault.
On the other hand, "beau voir" is also a set expression
in French, indicating cynicism:
          "oh really? I'd like to see that,"
or even,   "oh yeah, we'll see about that."

Hymenoptera

Ye cats that at midnight spit love at each other
Thomas Flatman

Fanatic,
keeper.
Lead the wall against all
and so
be a friend
of an eater,
a guest in the course of life
Lead battles
asbestos,
merciless
against life.
Yellow
in stereo,
sea
sponge
block flow
for sex.
Steal their livelihoods,
keep what must be kept
because
to antagonise
is outward.

Comfy

rat, o rat…
never in all my life have I seen
as handsome a rat as you.
Thank you for noticing my potatoes.
                    Christopher Logue

Why are antlers so sharp?
Because they're inconvenient like prison.
Pronouncing cities in the local accent,
the piercing of a tummy becomes a rattle.
A brown needle, some string gut,
all from the same old carcass.
The elderly won't admit it
but once you've seen one reindeer
it's always point-first antler up,
with splinters beneath a fingernail
and more endless work.
Fainting from the pain
with no idea which berries are poison
and which bits of the river are frozen.
Out here we're useless
like mire and roots rotting
on a beach.
We might as well be
put to use as glue
to replace their nails, severed
and black.
What use is material comfort
when the price is freedom?

Emahoy Tsegué-Maryam Guèbrou

Forgive me for having loved you because I can no longer tell you that I do
Liane de Pougy

A story of quiet survival,
a camp nun,
reclusing.
A lady even
toe
ungulate.
The eternal recurrence
translated
as a foil and friend.
A giraffe
that wears a collar
reminding each day
to be its last.
A name eats its leaf,
ceaselessly,
and is made
forever
the flame that does
not burn
improvised resonances
of Ethopia
where we were born.
From the river
a piano,
waiting,
without sight.
This is my memory
in detailed
sound.

Babysitting

(The Fox is heavy)
Geraldine Monk

Pretended to bite the dog
which wouldn't pretend
in biting me.
There's a mark.
A heart
is bloodshot,
and I am so animal
that playing greets me
as I worry about the fate
of interests that aren't my own
while others could care less.
Watching twitter,
I am a child's confidant,
but unlike them, cautious,
aspiring to be brave,
wide eyed and benign.
Like a miniature, fanged
fat cheeked doppelgänger
I have the future
and your ear.
In it drips poison,
rampaging in your brain
like some sort of enormous
aneurism catastrophe.

Fancy thoughts

Finally in a cavity below the diaphragm
a nest of young rats was discovered
One little sister lay dead.
        Gottfried Benn

I refuse anaesthetic, poking around the hospital
to find out if anyone will admit what they did to the guards
when liberating the camp.
People love dogs more than babies,
for in the former they cannot see their own origins,
because they actively emphasise
the concepts which are not reality
but help us manage it.
No matter what you say,
you have always been a family curio sold at a car boot sale.
You are happy, have an excellent disposition
adapted for dissection,
showering others with measured attention,
double doses of medical morphine at dinner,
emphasising the previously mentioned concepts
which strain living like a strap.
To roam the Tivoli Gardens,
fill gutters beneath the streets of Monaco,
to shit in the Jardins du Luxembourg,
to mate with the thigh of a wound, like a parasite.
This is the view,
in obsidian
seeing yourself as a man
ready for death
staring away, trembling
like a rat or a whale.

Where would I be without your love?

Drinking seems to me too much, too open.
Rainer Maria Rilke

Cloudy dog,
I am the animal called Anthony,
please let me in.
I am German, I am an able assistant for your abattoir.
It is too late to regret eating all those creatures
while patting your dog,
your selfless acts
a serious drought
against the blood
condemned to animal hell,
where I will be vivisected for days.
From my perch
I watch the inanity of humanity
pooling in its best shape,
expecting logic and reason
with a undented history of contradiction
and hypocrisy.
My heart is an olive on a saddle.
Government funding
buys my freedom
but while I pose,
I impress the ladies
with tales of fingers warmed
in your leaking light.

Careful of prayers they could be spells

at last I've done it!
put the white horse inside the carnation
        Tom Raworth

Blend that Lion. He looked at my feet
and said they were the feet he left in the cloakroom last week,
even though they are obviously my feet
and I had to give him them because he started crying.
Race that Lion. He talked to me when we bumped into each other
in the lavatory and it completely put me off and I couldn't go.
Fetch the boar. I am hungry for bacon
to surprise Livia. I'll have to get those chickens too, for the eggs.
Capture that dog. For a bit of flash when I go out for Igor's birthday do
next Thursday evening after work.
Fetch out the birds. They shit everywhere.
Fetch the cleaning fluids, clean the monkey stables. Obviously my job.
Fetch the bull, to generally to let everyone know I haven't gone away,
though I have calmed down, as it's natural to do so as one gets older.
Fetch the horses, so I can leave on one.
Fetch the girdle, there's weight been put on.
Fetch the soup for our guests, made of all the above.
Depending upon whether they are indeed as easy going and solid as
        people say,
we might also fetch the kids to guard my patio.

Death meal one at a time

I was tired again, with moderate-to-severe hunch pains
Thom Jones

Laying rodenticide
that looks like corn
so they'll buy it
from my stool.
Looks a legit business.
Too rigid to destroys beta cells,
causing instant diabetes,
free with poetry
it offers impaired intellect and coma.
Pity tracks this diabetic rat
with severe hypoglycaemia
like a homing device.
All will develop an incredible thirst for fat in time
and the sick cannot bear bright light.
Future life is a prolonged death of torment,
with shrunken thymus glands,
a swelling in the cranial cavity,
and shrivelling of the adrenal glands.
Yet some still drink huge amounts
and that's not us
in the final flicker
of all things,
its next. To my turn
I'm not looking forward.

What is bat and what is good?

and there aren't names for what it is.
when it disappears into its maze, only hope remains
that at least there are names for what it isn't.
      Aleš Šteger

Watch the road.
Watch it groan.
The carrot's give up as they touch brows
with the one
warm body
walking amongst them.
Orange crush
trailing
black dogs,
a fruit slipping out of those lovely puppies.
I owned one.
But I was a child
and those days have gone.
Newly rescued from a fire
a red
chair
full of newly rescued
human
being.
It wears a frown
which
appears a smile,
and vice
versa.
Its child asks the title question
to which it
answers
I've got you you little fucker stop squirming.

Is there a specific thing you have in mind?

Sorrow is knowledge, those that know the most must mourn the deepest, the tree of knowledge is not the tree of life.
Lord Byron

She walled in bounty
like the chocolate coin
that's a euro from Poundland.
All that's said best of that
is dirty and wealthy,
like Trago Mills,
joins in her face like dots under a pencil.
Joined parts, beyond that,
inside them.
Did they catch that manta ray?
James Gandolfini made it to 51
which waved in every strippers race.
A boat,
o softly lightens over the water.
How pure, how expensive houses.
And on that belly, and over that lips
so calm, so firm, yet loud,
The smiles that crush,
reject the light,
the drum comes in,
but tells of days
in happiness I've seen, a mind peaced
with everyone else's sexy moaning.
My heart whose love is innocent.

Oligarch

white bellied and good natured
wanderer of the captive deep
wild boar of the brine
                Thomas Prys

Eating a peach while stroking the royal fish,
who rests on a satin cushion
and inflates only to celebrate, and commiserate
the centuries end.
This was some years ago then.
Before money became bigger
and more easily accumulated.
It's hard for people now to remember what it was like
to not have so much of it,
it was strange.

The tiny lips of the fish whisper
it all happens for a reason
as something is buried alive,
as a contractor signs a contract,
as an addict to something dies
Beauty and humour are in this room though,
so you cannot blame the fish
for seeing what it sees.
My little hand grenade
my little bible popper,
so go the nicknames the man has for his fish.

This is the greek fish
who cheerfully stirs his masters moussaka.
A slow lovepact about power and cuisine.
Subscription viewers watch hungrily
as a fish makes revolutions in cooking,
as and when it can,
as though it were a wheel rolling.

Held in the tiny palm of a tiny claw,
raised to the sky to absorb the sun,
the pact is broken to avoid certain taxes,
though there are children to think of.

Aptitude

I'd like to paint monkey-eaters
like the painter who painted potato-eaters
Takahashi Mutsuo

At once at work, big full stop.
Repairing
dehydration
from a floret.
Its time
coded
visual poetry
and goes off if I leave the house.
I would gut the chat,
proud that the meat to killing
ratio were more 'real',
watching certain box-sets,
following football
and fingering its inner walls.
A fix it a small sensitive spot on the north face
and brim with pride
to sell
to the lost.
But a possession
for the dispossessed
will lead to crime,
fulfilled by things
upstream bound
which having never been lost
can never be found.

The song of back problems

I have no eyes
But my all-seeing wounds; and I am dumb
Edith Sitwell

Dinner
cannot cease
with bashfulness.
It's eating.
It writes to its student,
why have tea
when you can have revolution?
Then it asks it to dinner.
Play to win, it thinks,
a belief to go with feasting
and sleep.
Fortunately a tiny bib
fits perfectly
around a lecturer's neck.
They have forms
that grant permissions.
That acts as a first cause,
so it asks others
to eat
while it's still warm,
unless even that would be a waste.
        Don't touch, you're in charge.

Bribe track

You remind me of a brother but with too much love.
You're a dark poultry farm, a black ink spaghetti order.
You're a yellow badge, a purple balloon.
You're a nation looking down, while lovely numbers are looking up.
You are a Christian's patience.
I am myself, you say, *in all these tender little chicks,*
I am the last one – agile, fragile, indefinably edible.
Whereas, in reality, you are a skeleton with a nose.
You have asthma with its constituent shallow breathing.
You are an archaic way to meet future friends in the sickbay.
You remind me of Glenn Gould, moaning.
You direct the fish festival of Giudecca.
You enjoy the process, then you pretend the result is important.
You offer to collaborate with me,
and I must offset the unsettling forwardness of your enthusiasm
with an excellent website.
You remind me of *my* brother, or his story:
A drunk man follows two girls in an English city on a Saturday night.
Harmless, very drunk, he falls in the street, and they turn to laugh at him.
He's fallen with his body on the pavement and his head in the road.
A bus comes by.

The sloth

I'll lie down,
bright,
in my clothes of sloth.
        Vladimir Mayakovsky

The sloth lives in trees, harmless, I will grow lips to caress them.
The sloth hangs in the floods of harmful corrections, I'm kissing.
The sloth is awful to watch, really it is in public.
The sloth poses as the love of peace, said Augustine, knowing no sloths.
The sloth never poses, they are themselves trees animated.
The sloth pale throated to William Ansah asks *am I not a man and your brother?*
The sloth asks *is not good sense the companion of all complexions?*
The sloth asks *how can you treat me this way?*
The sloth living in man's coattails, sacking cities.
The sloth confused, a famous image, visited by many million pilgrims each year.
The sloth as a cropped ear.
The sloth as noblesse oblige.
The sloth with tiny fingers helping each human to cut themselves.
The sloth is hard to see in the mirror while cutting.
The sloth is brown-throated, maned, two-mandibled.
The sloth is pygmy and subterranean.
The sloth wrestles free of an ape's grip.
The sloth knows Gibraltar will go back to the Spanish one day.
The sloth pissing like Hanuman himself.
The sloth is his neighbour's god to be respected and tolerated.
The sloth is petty with the price of Paithan paintings.
The sloth has a taste for King Harishchandra.
The sloth is cursed to carry all horrors that retard humans.
The sloth is small like our habits, collecting footwear.
The sloth worries at worn hubs of slow divorce from the jungle floor.
The sloth always needs to go the toilet.
The sloth is sore smoke, ram headed and slight from worry.
The sloth has dengue fever.
The sloth is distressed by attention.

The sloth tries to cover your breasts.

The sloth fronts an ad-campaign advocating murder.

The sloth massages the salmon and its never-ending pink flesh.

The sloth tries to catch the heart-spotted woodpecker.

The sloth ties to catch the red-breasted parakeet.

The sloth tries to catch the pink-headed duck.

The sloth tries to catch the ashy wood pigeon.

The sloth can't.

The sloth is a rare bullet itching in its crimson casings.

The sloth claims a great prize.

The sloth is the fabled fiji mermaid, a monkey sewn tight to a fishtail.

The sloth has two toes.

The sloth administers a salt enema.

The sloth is a blue sunrise to cure haemophiliac's epilepsy.

The sloth is a pie.

The sloth is an anti-depressant.

The sloth has pope's blood on its hands.

The sloth is cheery darkness.

The sloth carves wet slogans into house bricks with its finger before
    it sets.

The sloth is a former union man.

The sloth has a lack of clothes, rejecting the trappings of life for a
    drifting path.

The sloth has scores to settle.

The sloth is a map.

The sloth mouths slowly *fuck you all*.

The sloth is not in the mood.

Bonus track

You remind me of a sister, but without the love.
You are a dark bonus, it's performance time.
You are the island pig dance with blood on the soft furnishings.
Yours is a supermarket poetry collection next to frozen squid.
I see a white badge, a blue balloon, a collapsing dome, a car crash.
I see the end of a friendship and am glad, it takes severance to realise.
My friends are looking up, while I'm speaking, looking down.
It's the me in all these tender little chicks,
the last one agile, fragile, indefinably edible.
First a pause, more news of friends connecting through invitation.
A punchline as timing, hammering fashion out of my own box
in the mistaken belief of networking as emancipation.
I am a troll with a nose. A skull with asthma.
A human skin suit I haven't visited.
An arctic way to meet future friends at the hospital.
I am director of the stuffed dog festival of Reykjavik.
I'll enjoy the process, then I'll pretend the result is important.
I'll offer to collaborate, and offset the unsettling forwardness
of enthusiasm with my partner's wonderful singing voice.
For no good deed goes unpunished.
You do your best to help people, and this is what you get.

Author's Note

With thanks to Tony Frazer for publishing poetry that has shaped my writing from the first, and doing so from the year before my birth until now. And for allowing me to join a tradition.

With thanks to friends and peers, Harry Man for his sage advice and production assistance, Lavinia Singer for giving me a book that gave me this book. To those whose hospitality I enjoyed in all sorts of places around the world while writing many of these poems.

With thanks to those who had and have shown me a good way to walk the path I've chosen, from experience, and with kindness, Tom Raworth, Lee Harwood, Tomaž Šalamun.